ME ENCANTA EL HOCKEY/
I LOVE HOCKEY

By Ryan Nagelhout   Traducido por Eida de la Vega

Gareth Stevens
PUBLISHING

Please visit our website, www.garethstevens.com. For a free color catalog of all our high-quality books, call toll free 1-800-542-2595 or fax 1-877-542-2596.

Library of Congress Cataloging-in-Publication Data

Nagelhout, Ryan.
I love hockey = Me encanta el hockey / by Ryan Nagelhout.
  p. cm. — (My favorite sports = Mis deportes favoritos)
Parallel title: Mis deportes favoritos
In English and Spanish.
            Includes index.
ISBN 978-1-4824-0853-9 (library binding)
1. Hockey — Juvenile literature. I. Nagelhout, Ryan. II. Title.
GV847.25 N34 2015
796.962—d23

First Edition

Published in 2015 by
Gareth Stevens Publishing
111 East 14th Street, Suite 349
New York, NY 10003

Copyright © 2015 Gareth Stevens Publishing

Editor: Ryan Nagelhout
Designer: Nick Domiano
Spanish Translation: Eida de la Vega

Photo credits: Cover, pp. 1, 7, 9, 17, 19 Lorraine Swanson/Shuttertstock.com; p. 5 Thomas Barwick/Iconica/ Getty Images; p. 9 Jupiter Images/Thinkstock.com; pp. 11/ 24 (ice skates) Victor Martello/iStock/Thinkstock.com; pp. 13, 24 (stick) Stockbyte/Thinkstock.com; p. 15 bigjohn36/iStock/Thinkstock.com; pp. 21, 24 (puck) Vaclav Volrab/Shutterstock.com; p. 23 (kids) Aptyp_koK/Shutterstock.com; p. 23 (gym background) photobank.ch/ Shutterstock.com.

Printed in the United States of America

CPSIA compliance information: Batch #CS15GS: For further information contact Gareth Stevens, New York, New York at 1-800-542-2595.

10 15

Contenido

Diversión en equipo 4

Sobre hielo 8

Juega con palos 12

Juego entre amigos 16

Palabras que debes saber 24

Índice 24

- -

Contents

Fun with the Team 4

On Ice 8

Stickwork 12

Friendly Game 16

Words to Know 24

Index 24

El hockey es
mi deporte favorito.

Hockey is
my favorite sport.

Juego en un equipo.

I play on a team.

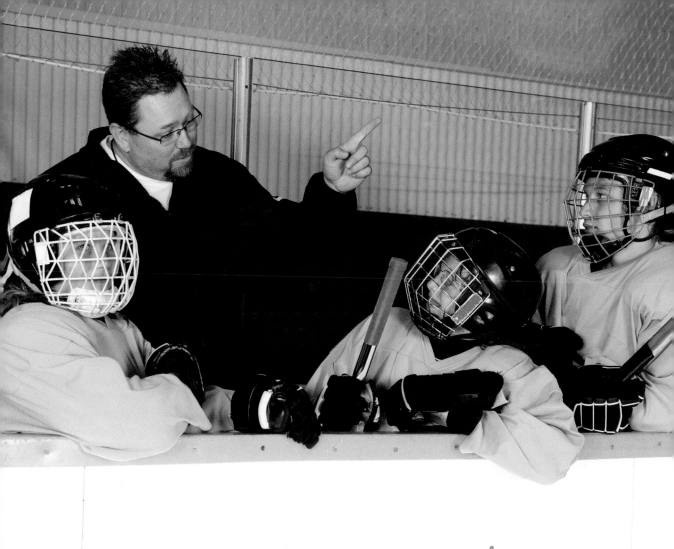

Jugamos sobre hielo.

We play on ice.

Uso patines de hielo.

I get to wear ice skates.

Uso un palo de hockey.

I use a stick.

13

El palo es de madera.

My stick is made
from wood.

Juego con mis amigos.

I play with my friends.

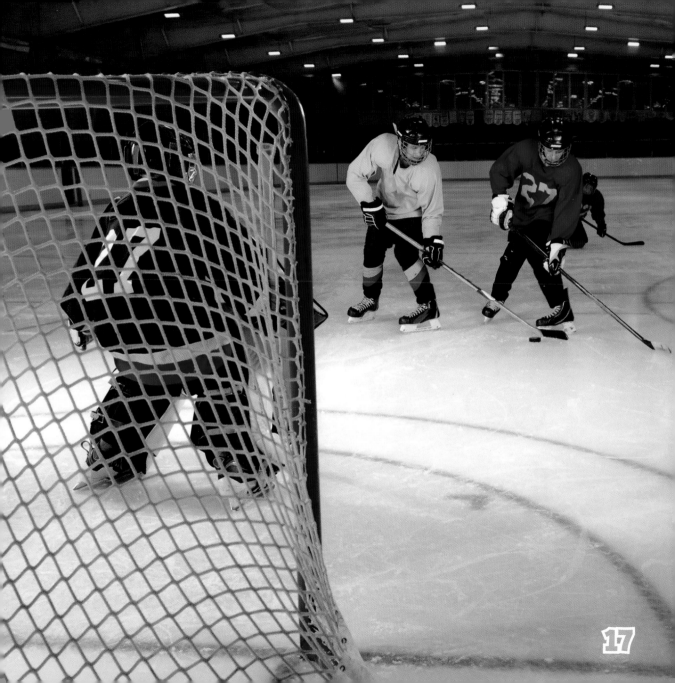

Nos encanta pasar
el disco.

We love to pass
the puck.

El disco es de caucho.

It is made of rubber.

También me gusta jugar
al hockey sala.

- -

I also like to play
floor hockey.

Palabras que debes saber/ Words to Know

los patines de hielo/ice skates

el disco/ puck

el palo de hockey/stick

Índice / Index

disco/puck 18, 20

hielo/ice 8

palo de hockey/stick 12

patines de hielo/ ice skates 10

24